Navy Atta

Spads, Scooters & Whales

René J Francillon & Peter B Lewis

Additional photography Benoît Colin, Ken Buchanan, Jim Dunn, Jerry Edwards, Robert S Hopkins III, Karl Kornchuk, Frank MacSorley, Bill Markell, Carol McKenzie, Rick Morgan, Masanori Ogawa, L B Sides, Daniel Soulaine, Don J Willis, and Marvin Yates.

Published in 1990 by Osprey Publishing Limited
59 Grosvenor Street, London W1X 9DA

British Library Cataloguing in Publication Data

British Library Cataloguing in Publication Data
Francillon, Rene J. (Rene Jacquet), 1937–
    Navy attack: Spads, Scooters and Whales.
1. United States Naval Aviation History
I. Title   II. Lewis, Peter B.
623.74'6'0941

ISBN 0–85045–969–9

Editor Dennis Baldry
Designed by Paul Kime
Printed in Hong Kong

Front cover Level and nicely centred, a TA-3B of VAQ-33 is about to trap aboard the USS *Kitty Hawk* (CV-63) during the afternoon of 29 March 1985. In October 1977, the 'Firebirds' of VAQ-33 added to their primary duty as electronic aggressors the role of Fleet Replacement Squadron (FRS) and Fleet Replacement Aviation Maintenance Program (FRAMP) for the A-3 community

Back cover A pair of A-4Fs from VMA-133, a Marine Reserve Squadron based at NAS Alameda, California, during a training sortie around Mt Shasta in north-eastern California on 20 September 1982

Title pages The Blue Angels Flight Demonstration Squadron flew Skyhawks from 1974 until 1986. Six A-4Fs neatly aligned on the ramp at the Naval Weapons Center China Lake before a demonstration on 27 April 1986

One last walk-around and its off to fly over the clear waters of the Caribbean Sea: an aircrewman of VAQ-33 finishes preflighting one of the unit's TA-3B

Navy Attack

Introduction

Between the spring of 1938, when Northrop BT-1s were first assigned to Bombing Squadrons Five and Six (VB-5 and VB-6) for service aboard the USS *Yorktown* (CV-5) and USS *Enterprise* (CV-6), and 1975, when Attack Squadrons 55, 164 and, 212 (VA-55, VA-164, and VA-212) made the last deployment with Douglas A-4 Skyhawks aboard the USS *Hancock* (CVA-19), aircraft designed at the El Segundo Division of the Douglas Aircraft Company were virtually synonymous with the attack community of US Naval Aviation. In particular, from the start of the Korean War until well into the Southeast Asian War, virtually no carriers deployed without at least one squadron of Skyraiders, Skyhawks, or Skywarriors. Moreover, with the exception of a detachment of Seasprite helicopters for plane-guard duty, the USS *Intrepid* (CVS-11) had only two squadrons of Skyraiders (VA-165 and VA-176) and two squadrons of Skyhawks (VA-15 and VA-95) when she spent 103 days on the line in the Gulf of Tonkin between 1 May 1966 and 30 October 1966.

There is no pretending that this book is an historical study of Skyraiders, Skyhawks, and Skywarriors—or, as they were affectionately known, Spads, Scooters, and Whales—in US naval service, or that it is exhaustive in its presentation of their camouflage and markings. It is simply intended to record some of these camouflage schemes and markings, mostly from happier days (from the photographer's point of view, not that of the pilot having to dodge missiles and avoid being seen by his adversaries!) when bright splashes of colour had not yet been displaced by effective, but oh so dull, Tactical Paint Schemes, and to provide a colourful look at three of the greatest aircraft designed by the one man who has often been called Mr Naval Aviation, Edward H Heinemann.

René J Francillon & Peter B Lewis
Vallejo, California, September 1989

Right Putt-putting about at 150 knots, 'Elecric Spads' from VAW-13 flew jamming sorties along the North Vietnamese coast and, not infrequently, over North Vietnam during the early phases of *Rolling Thunder* in 1965. VR710 (BuNo 132589) was photographed in the VAW-13 hangar at NAS Alameda in October 1965

Contents

Able Dogs

AD-6s of VA-35 from CVG-3 during carrier qualifications aboard the USS *Tarawa* (CVA-40) in the mid-fifties. The pre-1962 AD designation of the Douglas Skyraider gave rise to the Able Dog nickname *(Marvin Yates)*

Below BuNo 132506, an EA-1F of VAW-13, on a training sortie from NAS Barbers Point, Hawaii, on 5 September 1964 *(Jerry Edwards)*

Left External loads carried by this EA-1F of VAW-13 are from left to right an AN/ALT-2 noise jammer, an MX-900A chaff dispenser, and an AN/ALE-2 chaff dispenser beneath the port wing; an Aero 1A 300-US Gallon drop tank beneath the fuselage; and an AN/APS-31C search radar and an AN/ALE-2 chaff dispenser beneath the starboard wing *(Jerry Edwards)*

While equipped with A-1Hs and A-1Js, the 'Arabs' of VA-115 deployed twice to the Gulf of Tonkin, aboard the USS *Kitty Hawk* (CVA-63), from October 1965 until June 1966, and aboard the USS *Hancock* (CVA-18), from January to July 1967. This A-1H was photographed at NAS Miramar, California, before the war cruise aboard the *Kitty Hawk*

An A-1H of VA-115 of NAS Miramar in May 1965. During the war cruise aboard the *Kitty Hawk* one A-1J and one A-1H were lost in combat and two A-1Js were lost as the result of operational accidents. Three 'Arabs' were recovered but the fourth, Lt(jg) W L Tromp, died in captivity

Above Jerry Edwards, an ECM operator from VAW-13, stands proudly in front of an EA-1F from the 'Zappers' at Tan Son Nhut AB, Vietnam, on 25 May 1965

Right The deck of the USS *Bon Homme Richard* (CVA-31) during operations on Yankee Station in June 1965. Two EA-1Fs of VAW-13 Det E are parked next to the islands. Behind can be seen A-1Hs of VA-152, F-8Es of VF-191 (with 100 side numbers) and VF-194 (with 400 side numbers), and an RF-8A of VFP-63 Det E *(Jerry Edwards)*

Above
EA-1F of VAW-13 Det E on the deck of the USS *Bon Homme Richard* (CVA-31) in the Gulf of Tonkin in June 1965 *(Jerry Edwards)*

Right BuNo 134974, an EA-1F of VAW-13 Det E, sharing the deck of 'Bonnie Dick' with A-4Cs from VA-192 and VA-195 (respectively with 200 and 500 side numbers) *(Jerry Edwards)*

Above left The 'Knightriders' of VA-52 made three combat deployments aboard the USS *Ticonderoga* (CVA-14) before converting from Skyraiders to Intruders. This A-1H was photographed at NAS Moffett Field, California, between the first (April to December 1964) and second (September 1965 to May 1966) of these war cruises

Below left The 'Knighthawks' of VAW-33 sent detachments of 'Queer Spad' airborne early warning aircraft aboard Attack Carriers (CVAs) and Antisubmarine Warfare Support Carriers (CVSs). This EA-1E, photographed at Davis-Monthan AFB on 13 March 1967, had last deployed aboard the USS *Wasp* (CVS-18)

Above While assigned to Air Wing 14 (tail code NK) the 'Swordsmen' of VA-145 deployed to the Gulf of Tonkin aboard the USS *Constellation* (CVA-64), from May 1964 until February 1965, and aboard the USS *Ranger* (CVA-61), from December 1965 until August 1966. BuNo 142016, an A-1J of VA-145, was photographed at NAS Lemoore, California, on 16 March 1967 after the squadron had been reassigned to CVW-10 (tail code AK) for deployment aboard the USS *Intrepid* (CVS-11) beginning in May 1967

An NA-10 (BuNo 132598) at NOTS China Lake, California, awaits its pilot before giving a spectacular display of pyrotechnics on 16 March 1967

Above left For 12 years VA-122 served as the Skyraider training squadron for the Pacific Fleet. When given the task of training AD crews in July 1956, VA-122 was based at NAS North Island. In July 1961 the squadron moved to NAS Moffett Field and in February 1963 it moved once again within California to new quarters at NAS Lemoore. These A-1Hs were photographed at the station on 18 March 1967. Fluorescent Red Orange high visibility markings on tail and wings clearly identify the use of these aircraft in the training role

Below left An A-1H of VA-52 at NAS North Island on 27 August 1967, three months after this squadron had returned from its third war cruise aboard the USS *Ticonderoga* (CVA-14). The letter M is missing from the NM tail code identifying aircraft assigned to CVW-19. After converting to A-6As, VA-52 returned to the fray aboard the USS *Coral Sea* (CVA-43) in September 1968

Above During their third war cruise the 'Barn Owls' of VA-215 spent 112 days on the line aboard the USS *Bon Homme Richard* (CVA-31) and lost two aircraft and two pilots during operations over the North. One of their A-1Js was photographed at NAS Alameda on 28 October 1967, two and a half months after the carrier had returned to California

Right VA-122 in transition. In 1967–68 the squadron flew a mix of A-1s and A-7s before relinquishing its last Skyraiders to become the A-7 squadron in Replacement Training Carrier Air Wing Twelve. An A-1E and two A-7As are seen at sea during carrier qualifications in the fall of 1967. The carrier is believed to be the USS *Enterprise* (CVAN-65) *(Bill Markell)*

Above BuNo 132435, an A-1E of VA-122, being ready to be catapulted from the angled deck of the USS *Enterprise* (CVAN-65) *(Bill Markell)*

Overleaf The same A-1E photographed from vultures' row during a lull in deck activities *(Bill Markell)*

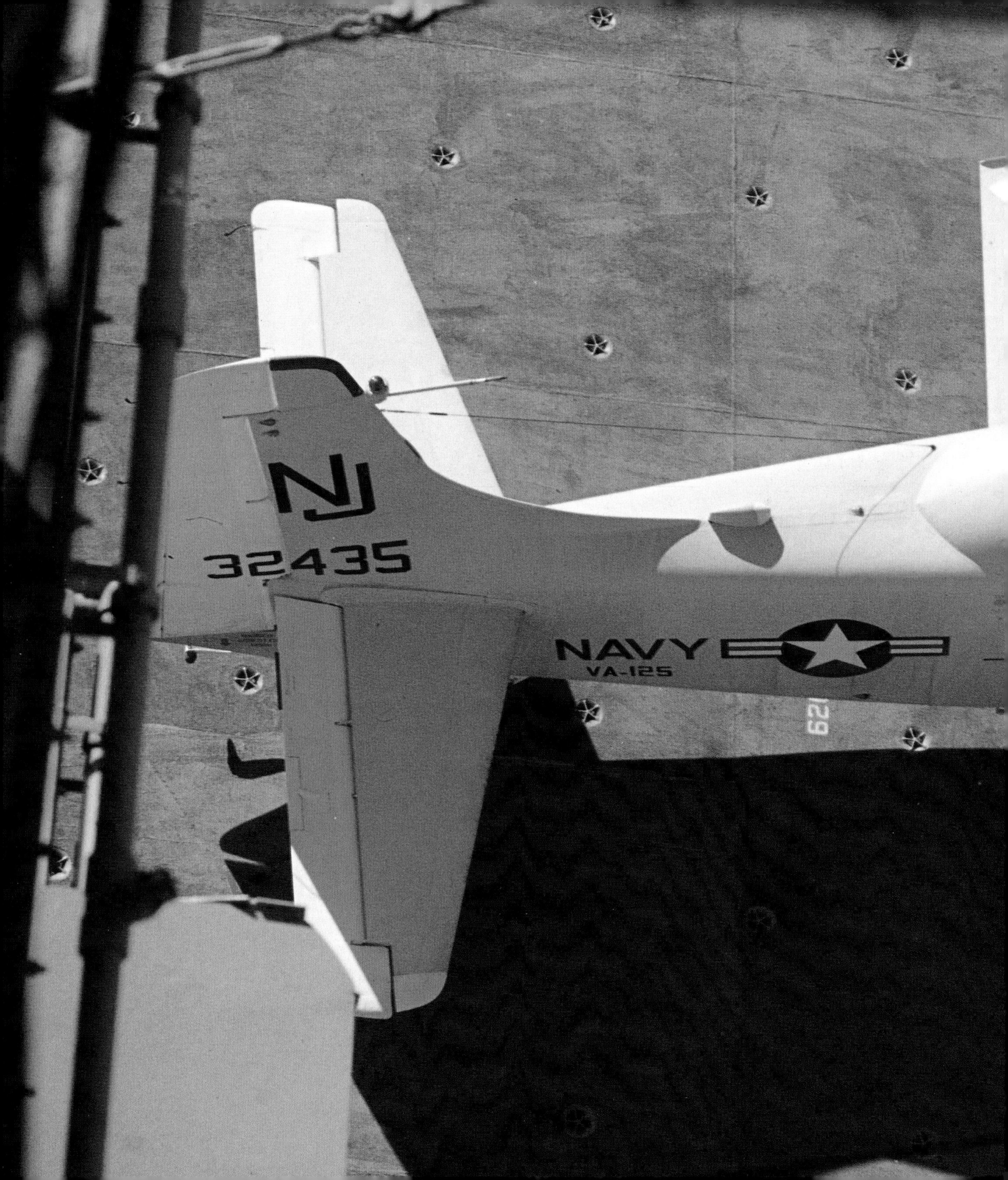
NJ
32435
NAVY
VA-125

While equipped with Skyraiders, the 'Wild Aces' of VA-152 made three deployments aboard the USS *Oriskany* (CVA-34). *Swamp Rat*, an A-1H, was photographed at NAS Alameda on 10 February 1968, ten days after VA-152 had returned from the third of these war cruises

Foo Foo Juice was another VA-152 veteran seen at NAS Alameda on 10 February 1968

An EA-1F of VAW-13 at NAS Alameda on 13 April 1968. EA-1Fs and crews from the VAW-13 Det 63 had embarked aboard the USS *Kitty Hawk* (CVA-63) on 18 November 1967 to make the 'Zappers' last war cruise with 'Electric Spads'. They returned to Alameda on 28 June 1968. Having received their first EKA-3B 15 months earlier, the 'Zappers' phased out their last Skyraiders during the summer of 1968 and were redesignated VAQ-130 on 1 October of that year

An A-1H of VA-25 at NAS Alameda on 13 April 1968. Flying from the USS *Coral Sea* (CVA-43), 'Fist of the Fleet' pilots had flown the last Skyraider combat sorties on 20 February when they provided air support for troops in South Vietnam

The end of the line: still bearing the markings of VA-122, this A-1E was photographed at Davis-Monthan AFB on 17 March 1969 as it was going into the Military Aircraft Storage & Disposition Center

Bantan Bombers & Tinker Toys

Left Skyhawks were assigned to three Anti-submarine Fighter Squadrons—VSF-1, VSF-2, and VSF-3—to endow Anti-submarine Warfare Support Carriers with limited air defence capability. Personnel at NOTS China Lake grafted the nose of a Grumman F-11 Tiger to this A-4B in an attempt to devise a low-cost air-to-air radar installation for A-4 'fighters' deploying aboard CVSs. The modification did not prove successful and BuNo145002 later had the standard nose fitted back. It is seen here with the modified nose while serving with VSF-1 at NAS Alameda in October 1966

Above A-4Cs of VA-113 aboard the USS *Enterprise* (CVAN-65) during training operations in the fall of 1967 *(Bill Markell)*

Wearing an experimental camouflage, this A-4E from VA-155 has been freshly painted in preparation for deployment aboard the USS *Constellation* (CVA-64) in May 1966. The fleet did not report favourably on the use of dark camouflages

A 'fighter' A-4C of VSF-1 on 10 October 1968 at NAS Alameda where the squadron had returned after a deployment to the Mediterranean Sea aboard the USS *Shangri-La* (CVS-38)

BuNo 156931, a TA-4J of VT-23. This version of the Skyhawk was specially developed to meet the requirement of the Naval Air Advanced Training Command

Above left The 'Warhorses' of VA-55 made no fewer than eight war cruises to the Gulf of Tonkin, one aboard the USS *Ticonderoga* (CVA-14) with A-4Es, one aboard the USS *Ranger* (CVA-61) also with A-4Es, one aboard the USS *Constellation* (CVA-64) with A-4Cs, and five aboard the USS *Hancock* (CVA-19) with A-4Fs. BuNo 155000 was photographed at NAS Lemoore on 17 November 1972 shortly after the fourth deployment aboard *Hancock*

Below left During the Vietnam War Skyhawks flew more defence suppression missions than any other types of navy aircraft. This A-4F of VA-164 at NAS Lemoore on 17 November 1972 carries a practice AGM-45A Shrike anti-radiation missile beneath its starboard wing. The 'Ghost Riders' had just returned from their seventh war cruise during which, operating from the USS *Hancock* (CVA-19), they had lost six A-4Fs in combat and one in an operational accident. Two pilots were missing and two were taken prisoner of war; the three other pilots from VA-164 were recovered

Above BuNo 148553, an A-4C from the 'Red Tails' of VC-7, ready for a target towing sortie from NAS Miramar in March 1974

Above left Beautifully marked CAG bird from VA-45 in transit at NAS Moffett Field in March 1974

Below left Composite Squadron Twelve (VC-12), a reserve squadron, was established at NAS Detroit, Michigan, on 1 September 1973. One of its A-4Ls is seen here on the transient aircraft ramp at NAS Moffett Field in March 1974

Above VA-164 was the only squadron to take two-seat TA-4Fs on a deployment to the Gulf of Tonkin before Congress mandated an end to US combat operations in South-east Asia. It is so aboard the USS *Hancock* (CVA-19) from May 1973 until January 1974. BuNo 152877 was photographed on 14 March 1974, two months after the 'Ghost Riders' had returned home to NAS Lemoore

The CAG bird of VT-21, with beautiful red 'tail feathers,' at NAS Moffett Field on 18 May 1974

The 'Saints' of VC-13 were established at NAS New Orleans, Louisiana, on 1 September 1973. They initially flew LTV F-8H Crusaders but quickly converted to A-4Ls. BuNo 149536 was photographed at NAS Miramar on 13 May 1975, nine months before the 'Saints' moved to this California air station

The JTTU initials painted on the fuselage side of this TA-4J identify its assignment to the Jet Transition Training Unit. It was seen at NAS Miramar on 15 November 1975

Inset Markings consisting of a black 'thunderbird' in a yellow circle were carried for a short period by aircraft assigned to the Naval Weapons Evaluation Facility at Kirtland AFB, New Mexico. This TA-4J of NWEF was photographed at Dobbins AFB, Georgia, in August 1978

BuNo 156941, a TA-4J of the 'Bobcats' of VT-24, photographed from the control tower at MCAS Yuma, Arizona, in March 1982. This NATRACOM squadron is based at NAS Chase Field, Texas, and provides advanced strike training

Left An A-4M of VX-5 aboard the USS *Coral Sea* (CV-43) in August 1982 during the filming of the motion picture *The Right Stuff*. For the greatest glory of Hollywood, the aircraft was being 'flown' by one of the future astronauts

Above On the occasion of the 75th Anniversary of Naval Aviation (ANA) in 1986, several NATRACOM squadrons painted aircraft in special commemorative markings. This TA-4J belonged to the 'Eagles' of VT-7, which are based at NAS Meridian, Mississippi

TA-4J of VT-24 in 75th ANA markings at NAS Pensacola on 9 May 1986

Belonging to the 'Cougars' of VT-25 this TA-4J was on the deck of the USS *Lexington* (AVT-16) when guests went aboard on the occasion of the 75th Anniversary of Naval Aviation in 1986

Basking in the sun and highlighted by the stormy skies of the Sierra Nevada, this TA-4J of Training Air Wing Two was photographed at the Reno-Cannon International Airport, Nevada, on 29 May 1988

Marine Midgets

During the South-east Asia War seven Marine Attack Squadrons took turn in flying A-4s from Chu Lai AB and Da Nang AB. Coded VK, this battle weary A-4E belonged to the 'Green Knights' of VMA-121. The Phantoms with FY tail code seen in the background are F-4Ds from the 555th TFS, 8th TFW, USAF *(Frank MacSorley)*

The A-4M, the last Skyhawk version built for the USMC, entered service too late to be sent to Vietnam. BuNo 158150 from the 'Bumblebees' of VMA-331 is seen here taxying at NAS Lemoore on 17 November 1972

An A-4F of VMA-223 at MCAS Yuma on 17 March 1973. During the South-
east Asian War the 'Bulldogs' deployed thrice to Vietnam, operating
A-4Es from Chu Lai AB between December 1965 and December 1966, March
and December 1967, and April 1968 to January 1970

Making good use of the ribbed, single-skin rudder of the Skyhawk,
Headquarters and Maintenance Squadron Thirteen designed attractive tail
markings reminiscent of the red and white stripes briefly applied to the rudder
of Marine aircraft in early 1942. This TA-4F of H&MS-13 was on the transient
ramp at Hill AFB, Utah, on 21 March 1974

Photographed on 28 January 1975, this attractively marked A-4E belonged to VMAT-102, the Skyhawk training squadron which was assigned to Marine Combat Crew Readiness Training Group 10 at MCAS Yuma

Above left A-4M from the 'Bulldogs' of VMA-223 at MCAS Yuma 14 May 1975

Below left Photographed in December 1975, BuNo 149614 is an A-4C of VMA-133, a Marine reserve squadron based at NAS Alameda

Above Sharing the Alameda ramp in December 1975 with A-4Cs with yellow and red rudders, this TA-4J of VMA-133 carried the same tail code but had a red, white, and blue rudder

BuNo 155006, an A-4F from VMA-133, flies past Mt Shasta, a snow-covered volcano in north-eastern California, on 20 September 1982. The fin mounted pod contains the aft preamplifiers and aft antennas for the AN/ALR-45(V) Homing and Warning System

Inset So long colours, hello drabness. A TA-4J of H&MS-42 shows the latest Marine fashion while taxying at NAS Alameda on 25 July 1982

Right Close-up of the Hughes AN/ASB-19 Angle Rate Bombing System (ARBS) as often fitted to Marine Skyhawks and Harrier IIs

Above An OA-4M (BuNo 154623) of H&MS-13 at MCAS El Toro, California, on 18 August 1986. Peculiar to the Marines, the TACA (Tactical Air Co-ordinator, Airborne) version of the Skyhawk was obtained between 1978 and 1980 when the Naval Air Rework Facility in Pensacola modified 23 TA-4Fs

The 1st Marine Air Wing is stationed in Japan but draws most of its strength from CONUS-based squadrons which are rotated every six months. Based at MCAS Yuma, this A-4M of VMA-311 was photographed at Yokota AB on 19 December 1987 during one of the squadron's rotations to Japan (*Masanori Ogawa*)

When this A-4M was photographed at MCAS Yuma on 11 May 1989 the 'Blacksheep' of VMA-214 had only a handful of aircraft in flyable condition as they were getting ready to become the first unit to convert to the night attack version of the AV-8B

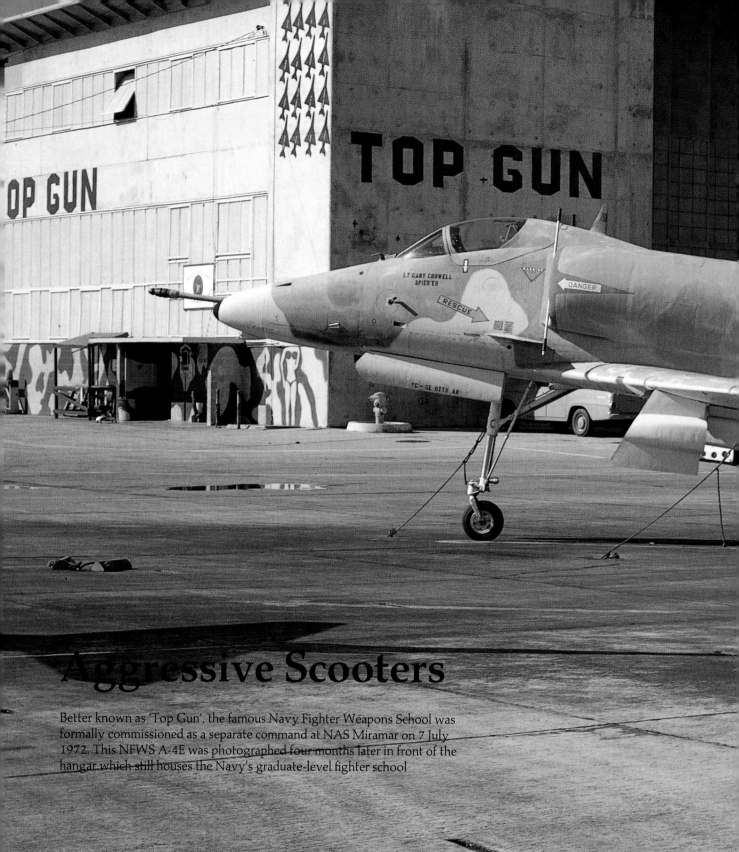

Aggressive Scooters

Better known as 'Top Gun', the famous Navy Fighter Weapons School was formally commissioned as a separate command at NAS Miramar on 7 July 1972. This NFWS A-4E was photographed four months later in front of the hangar which still houses the Navy's graduate-level fighter school

The CAG bird from VF-126 at NAS Miramar on 17 May 1975. After eight years as Attack Squadron 126 this unit was redesignated Fighter Squadron 126 on 15 October 1965. It received its first TA-4Fs in 1967 and since then has been one of the principal Navy adversary units

Above After functioning since May 1970 as the only Replacement Training Squadron in the Navy, VA-127 became responsible in November 1975 for providing training in defensive tactics against enemy aircraft to A-7 squadrons of the Pacific Fleet. For that purpose, VA-127 supplemented its two-seat Skyhawks with single-seat A-4Es and A-4Fs. One of the latter is seen at NAS Lemoore on 2 December 1975

Left TA-4J of VF-126 in bicentennial markings at NAS Miramar on 19 June 1976

Left BuNo 153483, a TA-4F of VA-126, taxying at NAS Fallon, Nevada, on 29 May 1981. The slightly raised canopy provides welcome cooling from the desert sun

Above An A-4E of the NFWS on display at NAS Moffatt Field on 6 June 1981

Two TA-4Js from the 'Saints' of VC-13 fly off the port wing of a KA-3B from VAK-308 before taking on fuel and rejoining the 'fight' over the Devils Playground in the southern California desert on 22 November 1981

Right BuNo 151095, an A-4E from the Navy Fighter Weapons School, ready to leap into the air for another dissimilar combat sortie from NAS Miramar on 18 October 1985

Below When the 'Cylons' began providing air-to-air combat training for Light Attack Squadrons of the Pacific Fleet, their aircraft retained the tail code NJ and side numbers in the 700 range which they had been assigned when VA-127 was a fleet-readiness providing transition training to A-4 pilots. Thus, the full side number of this TA-4J (BuNo 153690) seen in a maintenance hangar at NAS Lemoore on 6 August 1986, was 711. However, as is typical for aggressors, only the last two digits are applied Soviet-style on the forward fuselage

Above left Fightertown USA: A TA-4J (BuNo 153518) on the VF-126 ramp at NAS Miramar on 14 August 1986. The F-14As in the background are from VF-1 and VF-154. Flying A-4Es, A-4Fs and TA-4Js (including NJ603 photographed on 14 August 1986), VF126 has long provided adversary training through FFARP (Fleet ACM Readiness Program). It also uses T-2Cs to provide fleet aviators with an introduction to out-of-control (OOC) flight. More recently the 'Bandits' have supplemented their Skyhawks with F-16Ns and TF-16Ns

Below BuNo 155017 basks in the late afternoon sun on 14 August 1986 as it receives some tender loving care from two 'she-Bandits'. For use in the aggressor roles, A-4Fs have been lightened by removing the dorsal hump, wing root guns, and other unneeded equipment and have been re-engined with more powerful J52-P-408As. 'Super Foxes' thus have a near one-to-one thrust-to-weight ratio after part of their fuel load has been burnt

Above The end of another nice summer day in southern California. Most 'Saints' are already at the Miramar O' Club made famous by the movie *Top Gun* as this conservatively-painted A-4E of VC-13 (BuNo 150073) stands ready for the next morning's activities. NAS Miramar, 14 August 1986

Inset Fighter Squadron Composite Thirteen (VFC-13) is a reserve squadron based at NAS Miramar. It had been established as VC-13 at NAS New Orleans on 1 September 1973 and was redesignated VFC-13 on 22 April 1988. This TA-4J from the 'Saints' was silhouetted against menacing winter skies at Miramar in February 1989

TA-4J from the 'Fighting Omars' of VC-12 departing NAS Key West in the afternoon of 9 October 1987 as the sky takes on menacing colours before an approaching hurricane. The next day was rather wet!

Above A pair of 'Super Foxes' from the 'Bandits' of VF-126 at NAS Miramar on 12 May 1989

Right In between sorties, the canopy of VFA-127 aircraft are normally kept open to prevent excessive temperature build-up under the hot Nevada sun. *Ramjet*, as painted beneath the cockpit sill of BuNo 154334, is the nickname of Lt Ronald D Ramsey

For a fair number of its missions VFA-127 flies mixed formation of A-4s or TA-4s and F-5E or F-5Fs. No. 23, an F-5E (BuNo 160792), and No. 02, an A-4F (BuNo 154183), were photographed from the back seat of an F-5F as they were departing for an ACM sortie over the range east of NAS Fallon

Inset After moving from NAS Lemoore to NAS Fallon in October 1987, VFA-127 changed from Navy to civilian contract maintenance. Here a technician from Lockheed Support Systems, Inc. helps a 'Cylon' get into the small cockpit of an A-4F

From Spring to fall VFA-127
averages 14 missions/29 sorties, six
days per week, flying mostly against
air wings undergoing pre-
deployment training before
embarking aboard carriers. BuNo
154190 is seen carrying a Cubic
Corporation AN/ASQ-T13 Airborne
Instrumentation Subsystem pod on
the centreline station

Inset Aircraft 44, substituting for a
MiG-23, and 00, playing the part of a
MiG-21, go on the prowl over the
barren Stillwater Mountains in search
of F/A-18As of VFA-125

In June 1989, VFA-127 possessed three A-4Fs (side numbers 700 to 702 abbreviated 00 to 02), six TA-4Js (10 through 15), 13 F-5Es (20 through 25 and 40 through 46), and three F-5Fs (30 through 32). 00 was photographed from the back seat of 14 during the afternoon of 21 June 1989

Right Nicknamed *Desert Fox*, aircraft 00 is an A-4F (BuNo 154190) which has been modified for use as an aggressor, hence the absence of dorsal avionic hump and wing gun

Above Typically, a 'Cylon' flies three sorties per day, six days per week, during the nine busiest months of the year, thus accumulating flight hours at a rate far exceeding the NATO standard of 18 hours per month

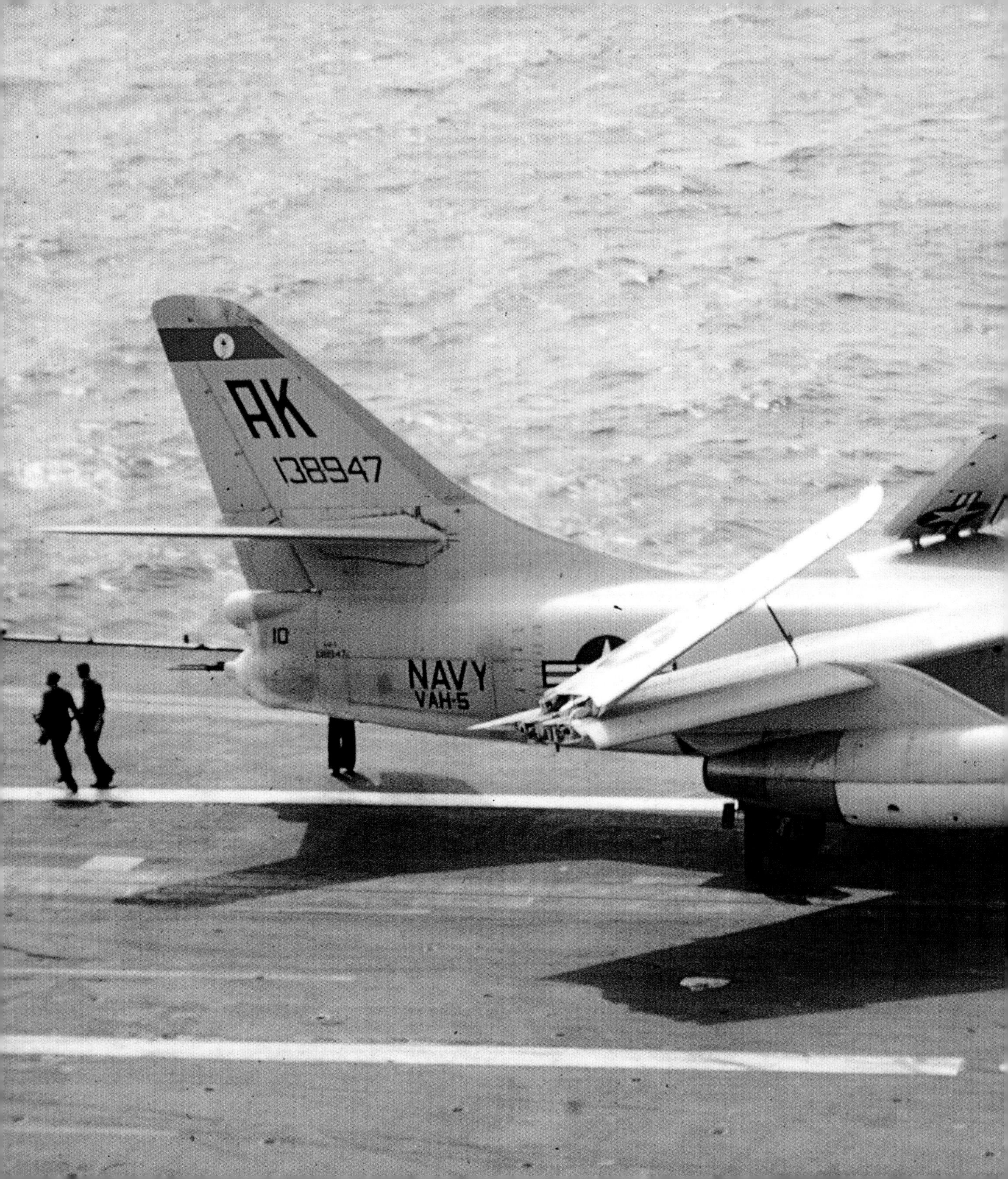
AK
138947
10
NAVY
VAH-5

A Whale of a Plane

Over the years, Skywarriors equipped 13 Heavy Attack Squadrons. The first, VAH-1, received A3D-1s in March 1956 and the last, RVAH-3, was disestablished in August 1979. VAH-5 flew Skywarriors for less than seven years during which it made four Med cruises aboard the USS *Forrestal* (CVA-59). BuNo 138947 bears the code of CVG-10, the Air Group to which VAH-5 was assigned for its first cruise aboard *Forrestal* between September 1958 and March 1959. Largest and heaviest aircraft to operate aboard carriers, the A3D had already been nicknamed the 'Whale' *(L B Sides)*

Right The 'Checkertails' of Heavy Attack Squadron Eleven (VAH-11) flew Skywarriors between November 1957 and July 1966. This A-3B was photographed at NAS Sanford, Florida, in April 1965, four months after the squadron had returned from its fifth cruise aboard the USS *F D Roosevelt* (CVA-42) and at a time when it had a detachment embarked aboard the USS *Independence* (CVA-62) for a cruise to the Med

Above An A-3B of VAH-4 Det 62 being prepared aboard the USS *Independence* (CVA-62) for a bombing sortie over the North in August 1965. Note that the aircraft carries mission markings for 10 previous bombing sorties. Later modified first as a KA-3B, and then as an EKA-3B, BuNo 142657 was lost at sea while being ferried from Cubi Point to the USS *Coral Sea* (CVA-43) on 16 May 1970

Above left After being damaged in a major fire while operating in the Gulf of Tonkin on 29 July 1967, the USS *Forrestal* (CVA-59) was forced to return home after only five days on the line. However, several of her crews and aircraft were retained in South-east Asia. This was the case of this KA-3B of VAH-10 Det 59 which was photographed at Da Nang AB in November 1967, two months after *Forrestal* had returned home

Below left Established at NAS Alameda on 4 March 1969, VAQ-133 made two deployments to the Gulf of Tonkin, one aboard the USS *Constellation* (CVA-64) and one aboard the USS *Kitty Hawk* (CVA-63), before moving to NAS Whidbey Island, Washington, in August 1971 to transition to the EA-6B. Seen at NAS Alameda on 24 October 1970, this EKA-3B was awaiting to go aboard *Kitty Hawk* and to depart for Yankee Station on 6 November

Above VAQ-308 was one of two reserve TACELRONs (Tactical Electronic Warfare Squadrons) established at NAS Alameda in 1970. This KA-3B (BuNo 138923) was wearing markings as applied initially to aircraft of VAQ-308 when it was photographed on 25 September 1971

This TA-3B (BuNo 144865) was modified as a staff transport by the Naval Air Rework Facility at NAS Alameda. It is shown in this May 1973 photograph bearing the markings of Transport Squadron One (VR-1)

Inset During the South-east Asian War detachments from VAQ-130 deployed with KA-3Bs and EKA-3Bs aboard nine carriers. Det 4 went aboard the USS *Enterprise* (CVAN-65) between June 1971 and February 1972 and aboard the USS *Ranger* (CVA-61) between November 1972 and June 1973. After the war had ended, Det 4 returned to *Ranger* for a WestPac Cruise between May and October 1974. BuNo 147667 was photographed at NAS Alameda five days before the start of this last cruise

The more discrete 'Queer Whales' (A3D-1Qs—or EA-3As after 1962—and
A3D-2Qs—EA-3Bs) have been assigned to two Fleet Air Reconnaissance
Squadrons (FAIRCONs) beginning in 1956 and ending in 1988. For most of
this time VQ-1 was homeported at NAS Agana on Guam while VQ-2 was at
NS Rota in Spain. Belonging to VQ-1, BuNo 146449 was photographed on 2
December 1974 at NAS Alameda after being overhauled at the Naval Air
Rework Facility

Inset Also bearing the 'Peter Rabbit' tail code of VQ-1, this TA-3B trainer was
photographed at NAS Alameda on 12 March 1975. It remained in service for
six more years and was the high-time Whale when in 1982 it was sent to
Vought to be expanded in stress and fatigue testing

Above left Bearing the yellow tail markings of aircraft assigned to the National Parachute Test Range at NAAS El Centro, California, this A-3B was photographed at this auxiliary station on 12 March 1976. During the following month BuNo 142242 was destroyed at the Naval Air Test Facility, New Jersey, during off-centre arresting gear tests

Below left The Navy Missile Center and its successor, the Pacific Missile Test Center, have made extensive use of modified Whales since 1959. This NRA-3B (BuNo 142667) was photographed at NAS Point Mugu, California, on 6 November 1977

Above NAS Alameda, 22 November 1971, BuNo 147660 being readied to take one of the authors on his first ride in a tactical airplane. Only the largest (yellow) helmet in the inventory was big enough to hold the swollen head of that bombastic individual! *(Carol A McKenzie)*

BuNo 147666 as seen from
BuNo 147660 during air refuelling
above the Devils Playground in
California. The shiny handle in the
lower portion of the photograph is
the D ring of the pilot's parachute

147666

XA-3G

NAVY

VAK-308

After refuelling BuNo 147660, BuNo 147666 banks away before rolling back its refuelling hose. As a tanker, the KA-3B could transfer up to 21,500 lb of JP-5 at a maximum rate of 420 gallons per minute

Inset Let's show the jar-heads how it should be done!' A pair of KA-3Bs from the 'Griffins' of VAK-308 tighten their formation before doing a tactical break over MCAS Yuma on 10 December 1981

Left Cdr George L Green, the cigar-chewing skipper of VAK-308, and fellow 'Griffins' stand in front of a KA-3B at MCAS Yuma in between two air refuelling sorties

Below Established as VAQ-208 on 31 July and redesignated VAK-208 on 1 October 1979, the 'Jockeys' of this reserve squadron were based at NAS Alameda until the squadron was disestablished on 30 September 1989. BuNo 146648 was photographed at MCAS Yuma in March 1982

Below The distinctive big nose of BuNo 144825 was fitted by Grumman in 1960 when this NRA-3B was being prepared as the test aircraft for the AN/APN-122(V) pulse doppler radar and AAM-N-10 Eagle missile control system intended for the Douglas F6D-1 Missileer

Pulling its billowing drag chute this KA-3B of VAK-208 (BuNo 147667 shown
in an earlier photograph wearing the markings of VAQ-130 in May 1974)
slowly returns to the ramp at NAS Alameda on 25 July 1982

As a tanker (that illustrated here being a KA-3B of VAK-308 at Alameda on 25 September 1982), the Skywarrior was fitted with a Flight Refueling A-12B-7 hose reel unit mounted in the aft portion of the bomb bay

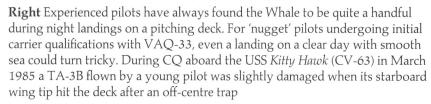

Right Experienced pilots have always found the Whale to be quite a handful during night landings on a pitching deck. For 'nugget' pilots undergoing initial carrier qualifications with VAQ-33, even a landing on a clear day with smooth sea could turn tricky. During CQ aboard the USS *Kitty Hawk* (CV-63) in March 1985 a TA-3B flown by a young pilot was slightly damaged when its starboard wing tip hit the deck after an off-centre trap

Above By the mid-eighties the Whale had become an endangered species and the sight of more than one on a carrier deck had become a rare one. Here, a pair of TA-3Bs are seen on the deck of the USS *Kitty Hawk* (CVA-63) during CQ off the coast of southern California in March 1985. One aircraft is ready to be launched on the No. 1 catapult and the other awaits its turn

Off she goes! BuNo 144858 is catapulted one more time from the
USS *Kitty Hawk* (CV-63) as VAQ-33 goes about its secondary business of
training aircrews and maintenance personnel prior to their assignment to one of
the six squadrons still flying Skywarriors in the mid-eighties

Above VAQ-34, the most recent A-3 unit, was established at NAS Point Mugu on 1 March 1983. In addition to Skywarriors, including this ERA-3B (BuNo 144846) flying off San Diego on 13 January 1986, the 'Electric Horsemen' fly EA-7Ls in the electronic aggressor role *(Rick Morgan)*

Above right The 'White Whale' of China Lake is the last Skywarrior to carry the A-3B designation. It has been in use at the Naval Center for many years and has been seen with various nose configurations as dictated by test requirements. It is shown here in standard configuration as displayed on 27 April 1986 during an Open House Day at NAS China Lake

Below right Assigned to Carrier Air Wing Eleven (CVW-11), VQ-1 Det C went aboard the USS *Enterprise* (CVN-65) for a cruise which started on the West Coast on 11 January 1986, saw the carrier and her Air Wing operate in the Western Pacific, the Indian Ocean, the Mediterranean Sea, and the Atlantic Ocean, and ended on the East Coast on 13 August 1986. As its crew was anxious to get back home to Guam, this EA-3B jumped ship and was seen in transit at NAS Miramar on 25 July 1986 *(Robert S Hopkins III)*

Around and around they go. Flown by a 'nugget', this TA-3B does touch-and-goes at NAS Key West on 8 October 1987

Inset Lt Dom Bouvet and a fellow instructor from the 'Firebirds' of VAQ-33 share a private joke while a 'nugget' preflights BuNo 144862 before a training flight off the Florida coast on 8 October 1987

Although marine biologists would dispute this fact, there is ample photographic evidence of the presence of Whales in the Florida Keys. A particular influx of Whales was noted in October 1987 when the A-3 community gathered at NAS Key West to celebrate the 35th anniversary of the first flight of the XA3D-1 at Edwards AFB. One of the guests was our old friend of VAK-308, BuNo 147666, which was wearing a new side number in the 500 range. Aerial Refueling Squadron 308 was disestablished at NAS Alameda on 30 September 1988

Speed brakes opened, an ERA-3B of VAQ-33 lands at NAS Key West on 8 October 1987. The wing pods are AN/ALQ-76s. Additional ECM systems are mounted in the ventral canoe, the extended cone, and the fin pod

Above NAS Key West, 9 October 1987: Three TA-3Bs and one ERA-3B from the 'Firebirds' of VAQ-33 share a corner of their ramp with a visitor from the sister squadron at NAS Point Mugu, a KA-3B from the 'Electric Horsemen' of VAQ-34

Right In the late morning of 9 October 1987, as the weather began to sour with the approach of a hurricane, nine Whales—including BuNo 144859, a TA-3B from VAQ-33—took off from NAS Key West for a 35th anniversary fly-by. All aircraft recovered safely but by the next morning water was coming down by the bucket full

BuNo 144843 has been the only Skywarrior to bear Army markings. Still
owned by the Navy, this RA-3B was bailed to Raytheon to be used at the
White Sands Missile Range in New Mexico for captive testing of the Patriot
(SAM-D) ground-to-air missile being developed for the US Army. It was
photographed at NAS Alameda on 24 October 1987 after being overhauled by
the Naval Air Rework Facility *(Benoît Colin)*